30 postcards

DARLING & COMPANY

SEATTLE

MMII

Classic American Children's Illustrators

This collection of work from fifteen American illustrators does not claim to represent the best, merely favorites of ours. All of the illustrations are from the collection of The Blue Lantern Studio.

Children's books have long been a favorite channel of escape and self-expression for creative people who retain a large portion of wonder and imagination from their childhood. Some of them find drama in the small events of a child's day; others like to break the bonds of everyday reality and escape into worlds of fantasy. In this collection Jessie Willcox Smith, A.B. Frost, Clara M. Burd and Sarah Stilwell Weber are clearly of the first persuasion. Johnny Gruelle, John R. Neill, E. Boyd Smith and Peter Newell are distinctly of the latter persuasion. All of these great artists see better than we do, which is why we treasure the records of their visions. Both groups tend to love animals, and we frequently find animals wonderfully portrayed in both familiar and fantastic surroundings. The other illustrators we include are: Lansing Campbell, Fanny Y. Cory, Palmer Cox, W.W. Denslow, M.L. Kirk, Howard Pyle and Frederick Richardson.

A big Hippopotamus
crashed after Uncle Wiggily,
crying: "I want to nibble your ears!"

LANSING CAMPBELL
FROM *UNCLE WIGGILY'S PICTURE BOOK*, 1922.

POST CARD

DARLING & COMPANY POSTCARD

TAP HERE

"Oh ho!" laughed the bunny.
"This water melon just fits your
mouth! Now let's see you nibble!"

LANSING CAMPBELL
FROM *UNCLE WIGGILY'S PICTURE BOOK*, 1922.

CARD

DARLING & COMPANY POSTCARD

TAP HERE

JESSIE WILLCOX SMITH.

CARD

JESSIE WILLCOX SMITH (1863-1935)
FROM SEVEN AGES OF CHILDHOOD, 1909.

DARLING & COMPANY POSTCARD

HERE

JESSIE WILLCOX SMITH (1863–1935)
FROM THE WATERBABIES, 1916.

CARD

DARLING & COMPANY · POSTCARD

STAMP HERE

PALMER COX (1840–1924)
FROM BROWNIE CLOWN OF BROWNIE TOWN, 1907.

POST CARD

CARD

DARLING & COMPANY POSTCARD

STAMP HERE

SOME HELD ABOVE SOME HUNG BELOW,
AND OTHERS WHERE THEY FOUND A SHOW.

PALMER COX (1840–1924)
FROM *BROWNIE CLOWN OF BROWNIE TOWN*, 1907.

CARD

DARLING & COMPANY POSTCARD

TAP HERE

A.B. FROST (1851–1928)
"BR'ER RABBIT," N.D.

CARD

DARLING & COMPANY POSTCARD

STAMP HERE

A.B. FROST (1851–1928)
FROM CARLO, 1913.

CARD

DARLING & COMPANY POSTCARD

TAP HERE

Great A, little a,
  Bouncing B;
The cat's in the cupboard,
  And she can't see.

FREDERICK RICHARDSON (1862–1937)
FROM *MOTHER GOOSE*, 1915.

CARD

DARLING & COMPANY POSTCARD

STAMP HERE

FREDERICK RICHARDSON (1862–1937)
FROM *FREDERICK RICHARDSON'S BOOK FOR CHILDREN*, 1938.

CARD

DARLING & COMPANY POSTCARD

UP HERE

PETER NEWELL (1862–1924)
FROM MOTHER GOOSE'S MENAGERIE, 1901.

CARD

DARLING & COMPANY POSTCARD

TAP HERE

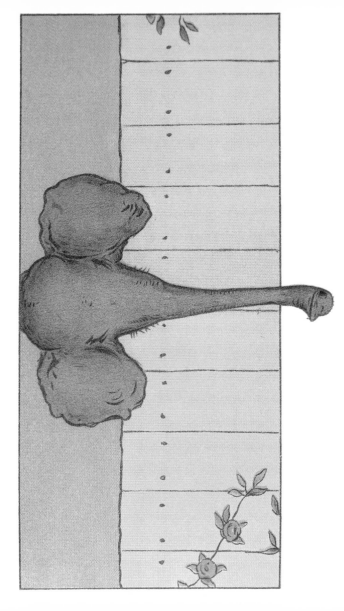

The Elephant leans o'er the fence and wonders why it is

PETER NEWELL (1862–1924)
FROM *TOPSYS AND TURVYS*, 1893.

CARD

DARLING & COMPANY POSTCARD

STAMP HERE

W.W. DENSLOW (1856–1915)
FROM *DENSLOW'S ANIMAL FAIR*, 1904.

CARD

DARLING & COMPANY POSTCARD

W.W. DENSLOW (1856–1915)
FROM DENSLOW'S NIGHT BEFORE CHRISTMAS, 1902.

CARD

DARLING & COMPANY POSTCARD

TAP HERE

E. BOYD SMITH (1860–1943)
FROM SANTA CLAUS AND ALL ABOUT HIM, 1908.

DARLING & COMPANY POSTCARD

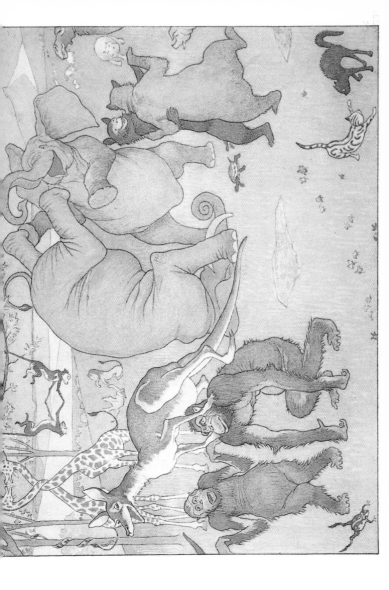

E. BOYD SMITH (1860–1943)
FROM *AFTER THEY CAME OUT OF THE ARK*, 1918.

POST CARD

DARLING & COMPANY   POSTCARD

STAMP HERE

JOHNNY GRUELLE (1880–1938)
FROM *THE LITTLE BROWN BEAR*, 1920.

POST CARD

DARLING & COMPANY POSTCARD

STAMP HERE

JOHNNY GRUELLE (1880–1938)
FROM *RAGGEDY ANN STORIES*, 1918.

CARD

DARLING & COMPANY · POSTCARD

STAMP HERE

SARAH S. STILWELL WEBER (1878–1939)
FROM *MOTHER'S HERO*, 1910.

CARD

DARLING & COMPANY POSTCARD

STAMP HERE

SOMETIMES·I·TOO·BECOME·A·STAR

SARAH S. STILWELL WEBER (1878–1939)
FROM THE MUSICAL TREE, 1925.

POST CARD

DARLING & COMPANY POSTCARD

STAMP HERE

POST CARD

DARLING & COMPANY [AE] POSTCARD

FANNY Y. CORY (1877–1972)
FROM JACKIEBOY IN RAINBOWLAND, 1911.

ǁMP HERE

POST CARD

DARLING & COMPANY POSTCARD

STAMP HERE

FANNY Y. CORY (1877–1972)
FROM *SUNSHINE ANNIE*, 1910.

JOHN R. NEILL (1877–1943)
FROM OZMA OF OZ, 1907.

CARD

DARLING & COMPANY POSTCARD

STAMP HERE

I
HATE
DIGNITY

JOHN R. NEILL (1877–1943)
FROM *THE PATCHWORK GIRL OF OZ*, 1913.

CARD

DARLING & COMPANY POSTCARD

TAP HERE

M.L. KIRK (BORN 1860)
FROM *AT THE BACK OF THE NORTH WIND*, 1909.

POST CARD

DARLING & COMPANY POSTCARD

STAMP HERE

COPYRIGHT 1910 BY FREDERICK A STOKES COMPANY

M.L. KIRK (BORN 1860)
FROM THE STORY OF HIAWATHA, 1910.

CARD

DARLING & COMPANY POSTCARD

TAP HERE

CLARA M. BURD (ACTIVE C. 1900–1930)
FROM *LITTLE MEN*, 1928.

CARD

DARLING & COMPANY POSTCARD

MAP HERE

CLARA M. BURD (ACTIVE C. 1900–1930)
FROM *ANIMAL STORY BOOK*, 1928.

POST CARD

DARLING & COMPANY POSTCARD

STAMP HERE

The Princess finds her Prince.

HOWARD PYLE. (1853-1911)
FROM *THE WONDER CLOCK*, 1887.

POST CARD

DARLING & COMPANY POSTCARD

STAMP HERE

HOWARD PYLE. (1853–1911)
FROM THE STORY OF KING ARTHUR AND HIS KNIGHTS, 1903.

DARLING & COMPANY · POSTCARD

MAP HERE

Miscellaneous Picture Credits

Page   1   Sarah S. Stilwell Weber (1878–1939). From *Childhood*, 1900.

Previous   Jessie Willcox Smith (1863–1935). Magazine Cover, 1906.

This page   Sarah S. Stilwell Weber (1878–1939). From *Rhymes and Jingles*, 1904.

Copyright © 2002
Blue Lantern Studio

All rights reserved
First Printing   Printed in Singapore

ISBN 1-883211-53-0

Darling & Company
Seattle